Fabulous Fish Re

A Complete Cookbook of Delicious Seafood Dish Ideas!

BY: Allie Allen

COOK & ENJOY

Copyright 2020 Allie Allen

Copyright Notes

This book is written as an informational tool. While the author has taken every precaution to ensure the accuracy of the information provided therein, the reader is warned that they assume all risk when following the content. The author will not be held responsible for any damages that may occur as a result of the readers' actions.

The author does not give permission to reproduce this book in any form, including but not limited to: print, social media posts, electronic copies or photocopies, unless permission is expressly given in writing.

Table of Contents

Introduction 5

1 – Char Fennel Salad 7

2 – Salmon Cakes 10

3 – Snapper with New Potatoes 12

4 – Tilapia Tacos with Slaw 14

5 – Orange Fish with Ginger 17

6 – Cod with Lemon Risotto 20

7 – Salmon Steaks with Yogurt Sauce 23

8 – Peruvian Fish Stew 25

9 – Steamed Fish with Ginger and Soy 28

10 – Nordic Salmon Salad 30

11 – Swordfish with Leeks 33

12 – Roasted Dijon Honey Salmon 36

13 – Parmesan – Garlic Tilapia 38

14 – Seared Ahi with Dilled Potatoes 40

15 – Garlic Curry Cod with Celery Salad 43

16 – Roasted White Fish 46

17 – Scrambled Eggs Trout 49

18 – Bass Bean Stew 52

19 – Soy Ginger Salmon 55

20 – Seared Glazed Ono 57

21 – Flaked Cod Rice Bowls 59

22 – Sea Bass Ceviche 62

23 – Whitefish Chowder 64

24 – Salmon with Zoodles 67

25 – Squash Salmon with Mojo 70

26 – Baked Cod with Basil Tomatoes 73

27 – Crispy Bass with Kohlrabi Salad 75

28 – Salmon Mushroom Bowl 78

29 – Grilled Sesame Salmon 81

30 – Brazilian Fish Coconut Stew 84

Conclusion 87

About the Author 88

Author's Afterthoughts 90

Introduction

What are the best ways to prepare fish at home?

Which method works best with what types of fish?

How can you be sure your fish tastes fresh and delicious?

Sautéing or pan frying is an easy method of preparing fish. You can coat the fish or leave it plain. This method works well with halibut, salmon, flounder and sole, among others.

Grilling is a popular way to fry fish, especially during the summer. Be sure to brush your fish with oil before grilling. Some fish that grill well include tuna, swordfish and salmon.

Many people enjoy baked fish. Usually, the fish are brushed with butter and often sprinkled with herbs. Dense fish works well here, like halibut, char and sablefish.

Broiling is an excellent way to cook fish, and almost any fish can be broiled, unless they are very large and are whole fish. Some of the best broiled fish taste comes from salmon and cod.

Lots of people roast fish, usually in roasting pans or on baking sheets. This method works well with red snapper, sea bass and trout. Try some of the fish recipes in this cookbook to explore the great taste of this healthy food source…

1 – Char Fennel Salad

When you slow roast char fish, it's almost foolproof, so it's a great way to get your feet wet, pardon the pun. It's easy to do and hard to goof up.

Makes 4 Servings

Cooking + Prep Time: 55 minutes

Ingredients:

- 1/2 cup of vinegar, unseasoned rice
- 1 tbsp. of sugar, granulated
- 1 tsp. of caraway seeds
- 2 tsp. of salt, kosher + extra as desired
- 6 thinly-sliced cloves of garlic
- 1 sliced fennel bulb, small
- 1 1/4 lbs. of char, artic, or salmon
- 4 tbsp. of oil, olive
- Pepper, ground
- 1 tbsp. of lemon juice, fresh if available
- 1 tbsp. of lemon peel, preserved, chopped
- 1/2 cup fronds of dill

Instructions:

1. Preheat the oven to 300F. In small pan on med. heat, bring the vinegar, 1/3 cup of water, caraway seeds and 2 tsp. of kosher salt to simmer, while stirring so the sugar dissolves. Remove pan from heat. Add the garlic. Allow to sit till garlic has softened a bit, 12-15 minutes.

2. Add 1/2 fennel. Toss, coating well. Allow to sit till fennel is slightly softened, 8 to 10 minutes. It should taste like it has been pickled.

3. Place the char in medium casserole dish. Coat with 1 tbsp. of oil and season as desired. Roast till the flesh flakes easily apart, 14-18 minutes.

4. Drain the fennel mixture and discard the liquid. Toss fennel in bowl with the last 3 tbsp. of oil, preserved lemon, lemon juice and the rest of the fennel. Season as desired. Add dill and mix. Serve the char with your fennel salad.

2 – Salmon Cakes

Salmon cakes are made with some ingredients you may already have in your pantry. That **Makes** them an excellent choice for weekday dinners, when you don't have a lot of time to cook.

Makes 2 Servings

Cooking + Prep Time: 35 minutes

Ingredients:

- 1 x 7 or 8-oz. can of salmon, drained
- 1 egg, large
- 1 tbsp. of mayonnaise, reduced fat
- 1 tsp. of lemon juice, fresh if available
- 1/2 tsp. of garlic powder, pure
- 1/4 to 1/3 cup of breadcrumbs, toasted, like panko, etc.
- 2 sliced scallions, medium
- 1/8 tsp. each kosher salt ground pepper

Instructions:

1. Mix all the ingredients together with fork in medium mixing bowl. Allow to stand for 5 to 10 minutes or so.

2. Divide the mixture by hand into two large cakes while pressing it together. You can add more panko if you prefer a crispier crust.

3. Heat butter or oil in skillet on med. heat. Sear salmon cakes for four to five minutes per side till puffed slightly and a lovely gold in color. Serve.

3 – Snapper with New Potatoes

In this recipe, the snapper is baked first and then finished by a quick broil. It **Makes** perfect, tender vegetables and well-browned fish.

Makes 4 Servings

Cooking + Prep Time: 55 minutes

Ingredients:

- 6 tbsp. of oil, olive
- 2 tbsp. of paste, harissa
- 6 lengthwise-halved onions, spring
- 1 lb. of scrubbed, thin-sliced potatoes, new or small
- Salt, kosher
- Pepper, ground
- 1 1/2 lbs. of snapper fillets, skin-on

To serve: lemon wedges, fresh

Instructions:

1. Place rack in upper 1/3 of your oven. Preheat it to 425F.

2. Combine the oil plus harissa paste in small mixing bowl. Adjust flavor as desired.

3. In large casserole dish, toss potatoes and onions with 1/2 harissa mixture. Season as desired. Add 1/4 cup of filtered water. Roast and toss once till potatoes become tender, 20 to 25 minutes.

4. Score the skin side of the fillets 1/4-inch deep and season them as desired. Rub the remainder of harissa mixture over all areas of fish, especially score marks.

5. Next, remove potatoes and onions from oven. Heat the broiler. Place the fish with skin side facing up on top of the veggies. Broil till potatoes and onions become tender, and the fish has cooked through and tops are beginning to brown, 8 to 10 minutes.

6. Serve veggies with fish and set out lemon wedges to squeeze over the top.

4 – Tilapia Tacos with Slaw

What could be better for a summer picnic than tacos with grilled fish? They can be made on the grill, in the oven or even on your stove top. The cilantro slaw adds an excellent finishing touch.

Makes 4 Servings

Cooking + Prep Time: 35 minutes

Ingredients:

- 1 to 2 pounds of white fish (tilapia, mahi-mahi, snapper, etc.), grillable

For the Spice Rub

- 1 tsp. of cumin, ground
- 1 1/2 tsp. of chili powder
- 3/4 tsp. of salt, kosher
- 1 tsp. of garlic, minced
- 1 tsp. of coriander, ground

Optional: 1/2 tsp. of sugar, granulated

- 1/4 tsp. of powdered chipotle (can substitute cayenne plus a bit of smoked paprika)

For the Cabbage Slaw

- 1 lb. of cabbage, shredded or thinly sliced, any color is fine
- 1/2 tsp. of salt, kosher + extra as desired
- 1/4 cup of red onion, nicely thinly sliced + extra as desired
- 1/2 cup of packed cilantro, chopped
- 1/4 to 1/2 jalapeno pepper, chopped finely + extra as desired
- 1/4 cup of lime juice, fresh + extra as desired
- 2 tbsp. of oil, olive
- Suggested garnishes include cilantro sprigs, chipotle mayo, avocado slices, lime wedges

Instructions:

1. Preheat a grill for med-high heat.

2. Rinse the fish and pat it dry. In small mixing bowl, stir the spices for fish rub together. Sprinkle it lightly over each side of fish. Set aside. You don't certainly have to use all the rub.

3. Place cabbage shreds in medium sized bowl. Toss with kosher salt. Add cilantro, onions, oil, lime juice and jalapeno. Toss thoroughly. Add more of these ingredients, to taste. It should be tangy.

4. Grease grill fully before you place fish on. Turn the heat down to medium. Then grill both sides for a few minutes each. Allow the fish to develop grill marks. Cook till done as you prefer. Squeeze with a bit of fresh lime juice.

5. Grill tortillas quickly on grill. To assemble tacos, place fish in tortillas. Add cabbage slaw and garnish with cilantro and lime. Serve.

5 – Orange Fish with Ginger

This fish is flavored with turmeric, ginger, chili and garlic. Sealing it in a pouch before baking allows it to remain extra flavorful and moist, since it can't dry out.

Makes 4 Servings

Cooking + Prep Time: 50 minutes + 30 minutes chilling time

Ingredients:

- 5 finely grated cloves of garlic
- 1 finely chopped serrano chili, small
- 1 x 3-inch peeled and finely grated piece of ginger, fresh
- 1 tbsp. of oil, olive
- 1/2 tsp. of turmeric, ground
- 4 x 8-oz. sea bass fillets, 1 inch to 1- 1/2-inch thickness
- Salt, kosher
- 1 clementine, small, peel only, chopped finely

To serve: lime wedges and cooked white rice

Instructions:

1. Place rack in center of your oven. Preheat it to 450F. Mix the oil, turmeric, ginger, chili and garlic in small sized bowl, making a paste. Place the fish on paper towel. Pat it dry. Season everywhere with kosher salt.

2. Use 1/2 of paste to coat one side of fillets. Place 2' sheet of foil on your work surface. Arrange the fillets with the paste side facing down, on 1/2 of foil sheet. Coat tops with remainder of paste, covering entire surface area.

3. Top the fillets with chopped peel from clementine. Fold other foil half over fish. Fold open sides over three times so you'll seal it, making a pouch. Place in refrigerator to chill for 1/2 hour.

4. Transfer the foil pouch to rimmed cookie sheet. Bake for 10 to 12 minutes. Turn oven off. Allow fish to sit in the oven for a minute more, allowing pouch to puff up a bit.

5. Carefully remove pouch from the oven. Allow it to cool for a minute. Then, carefully open it.

6. Transfer fish to plates. Spoon cooking juices from the pouch atop fish. Serve with lime wedges and cooked rice.

6 – Cod with Lemon Risotto

This tasty recipe uses real lemon to flavor the risotto with white fish. They are natural, wonderful tastes that go together well.

Makes 4 Servings

Cooking + Prep Time: 1 hour 5 minutes

Ingredients:

- 2 tbsp. of butter, unsalted
- 1 cup of finely diced onion, white
- 2 cups of rice, Arborio
- 1 cup of wine, white
- 4 or 5 cups of stock or hot, filtered water
- 1 1/2 tsp. of salt, kosher – use less if you're using stock
- 1/4 tsp. of pepper, white
- 2 fresh lemons, zest and juice only
- 1 lb. cod fillet (can sub halibut) – sliced in four pieces
- Salt, kosher
- Pepper, ground
- Oil, olive

For garnishing: lemon zest, micro greens

Instructions:

1. In medium pot with heavy bottom, melt the butter on med. heat.

2. Add the onions. Sauté for five to seven minutes, till tender.

3. Add the rice. Sauté for five minutes while stirring often.

4. Add the wine and reduce the heat level to med-low. Stir for five minutes or so, till absorbed fully.

5. Add 1/2 cup of hot filtered water. Still till it is absorbed. Continue to add remainder of water, four cups in total, while continuously stirring, till liquid has been absorbed and rice is cooked al dente. This usually takes 15-20 minutes on med-low.

6. Add kosher salt, white pepper, zest from two fresh lemons and juice from 1 1/2 fresh lemons. Taste and adjust as desired. Cover. Set aside.

7. In heavy skillet, heat 2 tbsp. oil on med-high.

8. Blot the fish dry. Season as desired.

9. Place fish with skin side facing down in skillet. Sear.

10. Reduce the heat level to medium. Continue to sear skin side of fish for five more minutes or so, till it's as crisp as you like it.

11. Turn fish over and cook for two minutes or so.

12. Add 1/2 cup hot filtered water to risotto and stir to loosen. Divide it among individual plates. Top with fish, skin side facing up. Top with the micro greens and lemon zest. Serve.

7 – Salmon Steaks with Yogurt Sauce

The yogurt sauce in this recipe works well with many types of fish or even with tofu. Here, it is paired with salmon steaks for an unbeatable taste sensation.

Makes 4 Servings

Cooking + Prep Time: 35 minutes

Ingredients:

For the grill: oil, vegetable

- 2 chilies, serrano
- 2 cloves of garlic
- 1 cup of cilantro leaves – leave stems on if tender
- 1/2 cup of plain yogurt, Greek, whole-milk
- 1 tbsp. of oil, olive
- 1 tsp. of honey, pure
- Salt, kosher
- 2 x 12-oz. salmon steaks, bone-in

Instructions:

1. Prepare grill for med-high heat and oil the grate.

2. Remove seeds from one chili and discard them. Then, puree the chilies with 1/4 cup of filtered water, honey, oil, yogurt, cilantro and garlic in food processor till you have a smooth texture. Season well using kosher salt. Transfer 1/2 sauce to small bowl. Set aside.

3. Lightly season the salmon with kosher salt. Grill them, turning a couple times, till flesh begins turning opaque, four minutes or so. Continue grilling while turning frequently and basting with sauce, till salmon is fully opaque, four minutes longer. Serve with the reserved sauce.

8 – Peruvian Fish Stew

This fish stew is made with a cilantro-based broth that is flavorful and easy to make. The carrots, potatoes and fish create a gluten-free, healthy recipe for lunch or dinner.

Makes 6 Servings

Cooking + Prep Time: 45 minutes

Ingredients:

- 2 tbsp. of oil, olive
- 1 diced onion, white or yellow
- 1 chopped ancho chili, green, fresh
- Optional: 1 chopped bell pepper, green
- 6 roughly-chopped cloves of garlic
- 1 tbsp. of coriander, ground
- 2 tsp. of cumin, ground
- 4 cups of chicken stock or broth
- 3 cups of water, filtered
- 4 cups of small potatoes, diced
- 2 cups of carrots, diced
- 2 bunches of cilantro, whole
- 2 pounds of seafood – fish, mussels, scallops, shrimp, etc.
- 1 tsp. of salt, kosher
- 1/2 tsp. of pepper, cracked
- 2 or 3 fresh limes, juice only

For garnishing, your choice: thin-sliced jalapeno, cilantro, sour cream, crusty bread to dip

Instructions:

1. Heat the oil in large pot with heavy bottom on med-high heat. Add the onions. Sauté for two to three minutes while stirring frequently. Add bell peppers and ancho chilies. Reduce heat level to med. Sauté till they are tender, stirring frequently, for 8-10 minutes.

2. Add the spices and garlic. Cook for two to three minutes, till fragrant.

3. Scrape all into food processor. Set it aside.

4. In same large pot, add four cups of chicken stock or broth and a cup of filtered water. Bring to boil.

5. Add carrots and potatoes. Simmer on med. till barely tender, 8-10 minutes or so.

6. Add cilantro bunches, including stems, to food processor. Add two cups of filtered water, as well. Blend till everything becomes very smooth. Set aside.

7. Once carrots and potatoes become tender, add seafood. Gently simmer till done as you desire. Add and stir in the cilantro mixture from food processor.

8. Heat to gentle simmer. Squeeze limes till the mixture has the taste you prefer. Serve in individual bowls with sprigs of cilantro, lime wedges, jalapeno slices, optional sour cream dollops and some crusty bread.

9 – Steamed Fish with Ginger and Soy

The steaming method for cooking fish is almost foolproof, and it works especially well with bass in this recipe. You can use the same recipe with cod, snapper or salmon.

Makes 4 Servings

Cooking + Prep Time: 40 minutes

Ingredients:

- 2 x 6 to 8 oz. bass fillets, black, skinless
- Salt, kosher
- 2 tbsp. of soy sauce, reduced sodium
- 2 tbsp. of sake
- 1 tbsp. of mirin
- 1/2 head of Napa cabbage – tear leaves if large, trim stems crosswise
- 4 oz. of mushrooms, mixed, torn in pieces
- 1 x 2-inch piece of peeled, thin-cut ginger
- 1 tbsp. of sesame oil, toasted
- 2 thinly sliced scallions

To serve: cooked rice

Instructions:

1. Slice the fish in six roughly even pieces. Season all with kosher salt.

2. Combine the soy sauce, sake, 3/4 cup of water and mirin in medium pot with a lid. Bring to boil. Reduce the heat level to low.

3. Layer the stems of cabbage, then their leaves, in the pot. Scatter the ginger and mushrooms over the top. Place fish on top of those. Cover the pot. Steam till fish becomes opaque and cooked barely through, 8 to 10 minutes.

4. Drizzle the fish with sesame oil. Top it with the scallions. Serve in individual bowls with spooned-over broth and rice on the side.

10 – Nordic Salmon Salad

This is the Scandinavian version of a classic known as a niçoise seafood salad. It's made with smoked fish, fresh vegetables and a delectable dressing.

Makes 2 Servings

Cooking + Prep Time: 45 minutes

Ingredients:

- 8 potatoes, baby

Optional: 2 boiled eggs, large

- 1 cup of snap peas
- 1 or 2 cucumbers

Optional: 1/2 shaved fennel bulb

- 4 to 6 radishes
- A bunch of watercress
- 6 oz. of smoked salmon or smoked trout
- 1 tbsp. of capers
- Dill, fresh

For Niçoise Dressing

- 1/4 cup of oil, olive
- 2 tbsp. of lemon juice, fresh
- 1 tsp. of mustard, whole grain
- 1 tbsp. of shallot, chopped finely
- 1 tbsp. of chopped dill, fresh
- 1/4 tsp. of salt, kosher
- 1/4 tsp. of pepper, white
- 1 to 2 tsp. of horseradish, prepared
- 1 pinch of sugar, granulated

Instructions:

1. Place potatoes in boiling water in pot. Simmer till they are tender, 18-20 minutes or so. Add snap peas to same water in last minute, blanching quickly. Rinse in cold tap water.

2. Boil eggs as you desire. Peel them and cut in half.

3. Stir all dressing ingredients together and blend in small mixing bowl. Adjust taste as you desire.

4. Lay watercress bed on bottoms of two individual bowls. Add your favorite toppings, fish and then dressing. Serve.

11 – Swordfish with Leeks

These thick swordfish steaks are firm enough that they can be cooked on med-high, much as you would cook a beef steak. The leeks prefer a higher temperature, so they end up juicy and sweet inside and smoky outside.

Makes 4 Servings

Cooking + Prep Time: 45 minutes

Ingredients:

- 4 leeks, medium
- 1 cup of olives, green, pitted
- 1/4 cup of dill, chopped coarsely
- 3 tbsp. of vinegar, white wine
- Salt, kosher
- 5 tbsp. of oil, olive
- 3 fresh oranges, flesh only
- 4 x 1-inch thick steaks, swordfish
- Pepper, ground

Instructions:

1. Prepare grill for high level of heat. Trim leeks. Rinse off dirt and sand, if any. Pat them dry.

2. Toss leeks on grill without oiling it. Turn every three minutes or so using tongs, till outsides have blackened, 10 to 12 minutes. Transfer them to platter. Allow to cool and reduce heat on grill to med-high.

3. Cut the leeks in 1/2-inch circles. Add to a bowl along with olives, dill, vinegar, 3 tbsp. of oil and large pinch kosher salt. Combine by tossing.

4. Remove skin and pith from the oranges. Slice them and set them aside.

5. Clean the grate of your grill and oil it. Rub the swordfish down with 2 tbsp. of oil. Salt as desired. Grill till charred lightly, and barely cooked through, five to seven minutes each side.

6. Divide the swordfish on plates. Arrange orange slices around them. Spoon the leek mixture plus juices on top. Lastly, drizzle with a bit more oil and sprinkle with pepper, if desired. Serve.

12 – Roasted Dijon Honey Salmon

The honey and Dijon flavors truly bring out the best of salmon's flavor. This is also an easy meal that you can even make on weeknights.

Makes 2 Servings

Cooking + Prep Time: 20 minutes

Ingredients:

- 1 tsp. of honey, pure
- 1 tsp. of mustard, Dijon
- 1 tsp. of vinegar, apple cider
- 2 x 4-oz. salmon fillets
- Salt, kosher, as desired
- Pepper, ground, as desired

For garnishing: chopped parsley

Instructions:

1. Whisk honey, vinegar and mustard together. Spread the mixture on the salmon fillets. Season as desired.

2. Place in 425F oven and roast with skin side facing down for 11-13 minutes, till a fork flakes them easily.

3. Remove from oven. Plate with fresh parsley and serve.

13 – Parmesan – Garlic Tilapia

The tilapia in this recipe is roasted in the oven and then quick-broiled to brown it. The parmesan and garlic truly bring out the taste of tilapia, which can be bland without special toppings.

Makes 2 Servings

Cooking + Prep Time: 25 minutes

Ingredients:

- 1 garlic clove, minced
- 1 tbsp. of unsalted butter, melted
- 2 x 4-oz. tilapia fillets
- Parmesan, grated, as desired

To garnish: parsley, fresh

Instructions:

1. Grate clove of garlic. Mix with 1 tbsp. of melted butter.

2. Season tilapia with garlic butter. Roast in 425F oven for 8-10 minutes, till fish is not quite fully cooked through.

3. Sprinkle tilapia with Parmesan cheese. Broil till golden brown in color. Dress with parsley and serve.

14 – Seared Ahi with Dilled Potatoes

This tasty recipe actually highlights the potatoes as much as the ahi. You can use halibut or salmon if you don't have ready access to ahi fish.

Makes 2 Servings

Cooking + Prep Time: 40 minutes

Ingredients:

- 8 oz. of potatoes, baby, any color

For dill sauce

- 1/2 cup of water, filtered
- 1/4 cup of oil, olive, light
- 2 oz. of spinach, baby
- 1 oz. of dill
- 1 chopped scallion
- 1 to 2 tsp. of lemon juice, fresh if available
- 1/4 tsp. of salt, kosher

For the ahi

- 1 tbsp. of coriander seeds, crushed lightly
- 1 tsp. of whole fennel seeds
- 1/2 tsp. of salt, kosher
- 1/2 tsp. of pepper, ground coarsely
- 8 oz. of ahi
- 2 tbsp. of oil, vegetable or coconut

Instructions:

1. Place the potatoes in small-sized pot and cover with filtered water. Bring to boil on high heat, then cover pot. Reduce heat. Simmer till potatoes are fork tender, 15 to 25 minutes or so.

2. To prepare dill sauce, place filtered water, oil and baby spinach in food processor. Blend well. Add scallions, dill, kosher salt ground pepper. Blend till you have a smooth texture. Taste and adjust seasonings, as desired. Place in small pot and set it aside.

3. Place the seeds, along with kosher salt ground pepper on small-sized plate. Combine well. Use this mixture to coat each side of ahi. Press seeds firmly in place so they stick.

4. Heat the oil on med-high in skillet till hot. Gently place ahi in skillet. Partially cover if seeds spatter at all. Sear on high for one to two minutes, till a golden brown crust develops. Turn ahi over. Cook other side for about a minute.

5. Heat dill sauce in pot on low heat. Warm it gently, being careful that you don't overheat it.

6. Place circle of dill sauce in center of plates. Slice the potatoes and place over dill sauce. Slice ahi and place on top of potato slices. Serve.

15 – Garlic Curry Cod with Celery Salad

The garlic and curry crisp used in this recipe is an excellent embellishment for cod. You can also use it on roasted veggies or braised chicken.

Makes 2 Servings

Cooking + Prep Time: 45 minutes

Ingredients:

- 2 x 6-oz. whitefish fillets, boneless, skinless
- 2 tbsp. of oil, olive
- Salt, kosher
- 2 tbsp. of clarified butter
- 2 thin-sliced cloves of garlic
- 2 tsp. of mustard seeds, yellow or black
- 2 tsp. of curry powder
- 1 x 1-inch piece of peeled, grated ginger, fresh
- 2 celery stalks, thin-sliced crosswise
- 1/2 thin-sliced red onion, small
- 1/2 lemon, fresh

Instructions:

1. Preheat the oven to 325F. Rub the fish with olive oil. Lay on cookie sheet lined with baking paper. Season as desired. Bake till fish is opaque and starts flaking, 11-15 minutes.

2. Melt clarified butter in skillet on med. heat. Add mustard seeds and garlic. Occasionally shake pan while cooking till garlic just starts turning golden and the seeds start making popping noises.

3. Add and stir in curry powder and ginger. Stir while cooking till fragrant, 15-20 seconds. Remove from the heat.

4. Toss onions and celery in small sized bowl. Grate zest finely. Squeeze in lemon juice. Combine by tossing.

5. Divide fish between two plates. Spoon the curry with garlic on top. Add celery salad and serve.

16 – Roasted White Fish

This is a healthy, simple recipe for mustard seed fish with hash made from Brussels sprouts and potatoes. It's filled with flavor and easy to make.

Makes 2 Servings

Cooking + Prep Time: 50 minutes

Ingredients:

For hash

- 8 to 10 oz. of thin-sliced potatoes
- 1 thin-sliced shallot, large
- 1 tbsp. of oil, olive
- Salt, kosher, as desired
- Pepper, ground, as desired
- 8 oz. of thin-sliced Brussels sprouts, fresh

Optional: a pinch of caraway seeds

For fish

- 2 x 6-oz. fish fillets (you can substitute tofu or chicken breast if you like)
- 2 to 4 tsp. of mustard, whole grain
- 2 tsp. of oil, olive
- Salt, kosher, as desired
- Pepper, ground, as desired

Instructions:

1. Preheat the oven to 450 degrees F.

2. Slice shallots and potatoes. Then, toss with olive oil and season as desired. Place on cookie sheet lined with baking paper in one layer. Bake for 18-20 minutes.

3. Slice Brussels sprouts. Place in same, oiled bowl. Toss. Add pinch caraway seeds and season as desired. Set bowl aside.

4. Mix oil and mustard together in small mixing bowl. Season fish as desired. Divide mustard mixture and spoon over fish.

5. When potatoes have been baking for 20 minutes, add Brussels sprouts. Toss briefly. Lay fish into the mixture. Bake for 10 t0 12 minutes more, till fish has cooked fully through.

6. Divide hash in two individual-sized bowls. Top with glazed fish and serve.

17 – Scrambled Eggs Trout

If you'd like making egg toasts like they do in restaurants, this recipe will show you how. High quality bread and fish will make this a winning dish.

Makes 4 Servings

Cooking + Prep Time: 55 minutes

Ingredients:

- 8 eggs, large
- 3/4 tsp. of salt, kosher + extra as desired
- 6 tbsp. of butter, unsalted
- 4 x 1-inch thick slices of bread, country-style or sourdough
- 3 tbsp. of sour cream or crème fraiche
- 1 trout fillet, smoked, boneless, de-skinned, flesh broken in 1-inch pieces
- 1 halved lemon, fresh
- Pepper, ground
- 2 diagonally thin-sliced scallions, medium
- 2 tbsp. of dill, chopped coarsely
- 4 oz of arugula, mature – trim away tough stems
- 2 tsp. of oil, olive

Instructions:

1. Crack the eggs in medium mixing bowl. Add 3/4 tsp. of kosher salt. Whisk till there are not any streaks remaining.

2. Heat 2 tbsp. of butter in non-stick skillet on med. heat. When foaming stops, add two slices bread. Cook till underneath is golden brown, three minutes. Transfer bread to plates with the cooked sides facing up. Repeat with 2 more tbsp. of butter and last two bread slices. Wipe skillet and allow it to cool for three minutes.

3. Heat the last 2 tbsp. of butter in same skillet on med-low. Once the butter foams, cook the egg mixture till curds start forming but eggs themselves still are runny, two minutes or so. Stir in the crème fraiche or sour cream. Stir occasionally while cooking till eggs have just set, one minute or so.

4. Spoon the eggs over pieces of toast. Top them with the trout. Grate lemon zest finely from one lemon half. Squeeze juice on toast. Season with ground pepper and scatter dill and scallions over the top.

5. Squeeze the juice from remaining half of lemon in medium mixing bowl. Add the arugula. Drizzle with the oil. Season as desired and toss, coating well. Mound beside the toast. Serve.

18 – Bass Bean Stew

These ingredients come together easily, making a savory, satisfying meal. You can used canned beans if you want to make the recipe more quickly.

Makes 2-4 Servings

Cooking + Prep Time: 35 minutes

Ingredients:

- 2 tbsp. of oil, olive
- 1 diced onion, medium
- 2 peeled and diced carrots, medium
- 2 stalks of celery, diced
- 3 or 4 rough-chopped, smashed cloves of garlic
- 2 cups of tomatoes, diced
- 3 cups of cannellini beans (can substitute 2 cans of rinsed, drained beans)
- 4 cups of stock, chicken
- 1 to 2 cups of water, filtered
- 2 tbsp. of sage, fresh
- 1/2 tsp. of salt, kosher
- 1/4 tsp. of pepper, cracked
- 4 x 4-oz. fillets, bass (can substitute cod or halibut)

For fish: olive oil, kosher salt ground pepper

For garnishing: parsley, Italian if available

Instructions:

1. Soak dried beans overnight, if using.

2. In large-sized heavy pot, heat the oil on med-high. Add the onions. Stir for a couple minutes. Add garlic, carrots and celery. Reduce heat level down to med. Sauté for three to five minutes while occasionally stirring.

3. After carrots, garlic and celery have sautéed for five minutes, add beans and stock. Add a couple extra cups of filtered water. Add herbs. Bring to boil over high heat.

4. Cover pot. Reduce heat level to low. Allow to simmer for two hours. Add kosher salt, ground pepper tomatoes. Continue to simmer for 1/2 hour longer.

5. Heat 1 to 2 tbsp. oil in heavy skillet on med-high. Pat fish dry using paper towels. Season as desired. Sear both sides till they have golden crust. Reduce heat and cook till done as you desire. Don't overcook the fish.

6. Place stew in shallow, wide bowl. Top with the seared fish. Use parsley to garnish. Serve.

19 – Soy Ginger Salmon

This is my family's favorite salmon recipe of all. The sweet ginger glaze perfectly complements the natural goodness of salmon.

Makes 2 Servings

Cooking + Prep Time: 20 minutes

Ingredients:

- 1 tbsp. of oil, olive
- 1 tsp. of ginger, minced, fresh
- 1 tsp. of soy sauce, low sodium
- 2 x 4-oz. salmon fillets
- Salt, kosher
- Pepper, ground
- Scallions, chopped

Instructions:

1. Heat oil in non-stick skillet on med. heat till it shimmers.

2. Season the salmon as desired. Sear with skin side facing up for three to four minutes. Flip and top with a bit of minced ginger and 1 tsp. soy sauce. Cook for three to five minutes more.

3. When fish will easily flake with fork, remove from heat. Top with scallions and serve.

20 – Seared Glazed Ono

The ono fish recipe is light and refreshing, with satisfying, clean flavors. Ono is a flaky, delicate fish with a mild flavor, and it tastes best grilled or seared to a med-rare level.

Makes 4-6 Servings

Cooking + Prep Time: 35 minutes

Ingredients:

- 1 1/2 pounds of ono, fresh, cut in four to six pieces (can sub tuna or scallops)
- 1/3 cup of low sodium soy sauce
- 1/3 cup of honey, pure
- 3 tbsp. of ginger, sliced
- 2 cloves of garlic
- 1 tbsp. of oil, olive

Instructions:

1. To prepare marinade, blend the soy sauce with honey, oil, ginger and garlic in food processor till smooth. Place marinade and fish in zipper top plastic bag for minimum of 20 minutes, maximum of 24 hours.

2. Heat the oil in large skillet on med-high. When oil has heated, place fish in skillet and save remainder of marinade. Sear fish and set them aside.

3. Pour remainder of marinade into skillet. Bring to boil for 1/2 minute till it has thickened. Strain. Pour in small sized bowl.

4. Spoon marinade over fish. Serve.

21 – Flaked Cod Rice Bowls

This recipe sometimes utilizes smoked fish, but steaming is easier for light weeknight meals. The fish can be steamed atop the rice if you wish.

Makes 2 Servings

Cooking + Prep Time: 55 minutes

Ingredients:

- 2 eggs, large
- 2 tbsp. of oil, olive
- 2 crushed cloves of garlic
- 1 tsp. of curry powder
- 3/4 cup of rinsed, drained rice, basmati
- 2 x 5 to 6 oz. cod fillets
- Salt, kosher
- 1/4 cup of whole milk yogurt, Greek
- 1 thinly sliced celery stalk
- 1/2 cup of cilantro leaves, including the tender stems

To serve: lime wedges, fresh

Instructions:

1. Cook the eggs in small pan of bubbling water for eight to 10 minutes. Transfer to medium-sized bowl with cold water. Allow to cool till barely warm, three minutes or so. Peel and set them aside.

2. Next, heat oil in large pan on medium heat. Then cook the garlic while occasionally tossing, till it has browned lightly, four to five minutes. Add the curry powder, 1 1/4 cups of water and the rice. Bring to simmer. Cover and reduce the heat level to low. Cook till rice is almost tender, 12-15 minutes.

3. Generously season the fish with kosher salt and one pinch curry powder, as desired. Then lay the fish on the rice. Cover and continue cooking till rice becomes tender and the fish will flake apart when you poke it with a fork, approximately 8 to 10 minutes.

4. Divide the yogurt among individual bowls. Top with rice and fish. Halve the eggs and then arrange them alongside. Use cilantro and celery to top. Serve with lime wedges.

22 – Sea Bass Ceviche

This delicious ceviche recipe is simple to make and very popular in our home. It's made with fresh fish, tomatoes, cucumbers, lime, chilies and cilantro.

Makes 6 Servings

Cooking + Prep Time: 1 hour

Ingredients:

- 1/2 thin-sliced onion, red
- 1 lb. x 1/2" cubed bass, fresh (you can substitute tilapia or mahi mahi)
- 2 or 3 minced cloves of garlic
- 1 to 1 1/2 tsp. of kosher salt + more if desired
- 1/4 tsp. of pepper, black
- 1/4 to 1/2 cup of nicely chopped cilantro, fresh
- 1 serrano pepper, fresh, de-seeded and chopped finely
- 3/4 cup of lime juice, fresh squeezed if available
- 1 cup of halved tomatoes, cherry
- 1 cup of cucumber, diced

Optional: 1 tbsp. of oil, olive

Instructions:

1. Slice onion thinly. Generously salt and allow to stand for 10-15 minutes till it starts releasing its liquid, which will make it less bitter. Rinse and squeeze onion slices dry.

2. Place the fish, onions, garlic, chilies, lime juice, kosher salt ground pepper in large, shallow bowl. Mix gently. Place in refrigerator and marinate for 1/2 hour minimum. The longer the better when it comes to marinating for this dish.

3. Toss in tomatoes, cilantro and cucumbers. Drizzle with oil. Mix gently. Season as desired and serve.

23 – Whitefish Chowder

The tasty stock makes a world of difference in this smooth, savory chowder. Select the best fillets, preferably deboned at a fish market, to make the recipe easier at home.

Makes 8 Servings

Cooking + Prep Time: 45 minutes

Ingredients:

- 12 cups of water, filtered
- Stock, fish

For the Stew:

- 1 pound of quartered potatoes, Yukon Gold, small
- Salt, kosher
- 1 lengthwise-halved, crosswise-sliced bulb of fennel – reserve the fronds for serving
- 1 1/2 x 1-inch cut white fish (cod is a good choice), skinless, boneless
- 2 cups of tomatoes, ripe

To drizzle: oil, olive

- Pepper, ground

Instructions:

1. Mix water and stock in large pot. Cook till fluid has reduced.

2. Place the potatoes and fish stock in large pot. Season with kosher salt. Bring to boil. Reduce the heat level to medium and bring to simmer. Stir occasionally while cooking till potatoes are nearly tender, 10-15 minutes.

3. Add white parts of leeks and sliced fennel. Stir occasionally and cook till veggies are just tender, four to six minutes. Add the fish. Cook till fish turns opaque, three to four minutes. Remove pot from the heat. Stir in the tomatoes. Adjust the seasoning as desired.

4. Ladle the chowder in individual bowls. Top with fronds of fennel. Use oil to drizzle and season with ground pepper. Serve.

24 – Salmon with Zoodles

This healthy, easy salmon recipe is served on lemon-y zoodles, which are zucchini spiralized or grated into noodle shapes. It's topped with summer-sweet tomatoes for a delicious meal.

Makes 2 Servings

Cooking + Prep Time: 35 minutes

Ingredients:

- 8 to 10 oz. of salmon (can sub halibut, cod or tofu)
- 1 smashed clove of garlic
- 1 to 2 tbsp. of oil, olive
- Salt, sea, as desired
- Pepper, ground, as desired

For zoodles

- 1 tbsp. of oil, olive
- 1 thinly sliced shallot
- 3 chopped cloves of garlic
- 12 to 16 oz. of zoodles – zucchini noodles
- Salt, sea, as desired
- Pepper, ground, as desired
- 2 tsp. of zest, lemon
- 1/2 cup of parsley, chopped
- 1 tbsp. of lemon juice, fresh if available, add more as desired

Instructions:

1. Preheat the oven to 375 degrees F.

2. Heat the oil in skillet on med. heat. Add garlic. Swirl, infusing the garlic into oil.

3. Pat the fish dry. Season as desired. Sear each side till golden in color. Place in oven till cooked as you desire, typically three to six minutes or so.

4. In large sized skillet, heat additional oil on med. heat. Add 3 chopped garlic cloves and shallots. Stir till fragrant and softened, two to three minutes.

5. Slice zucchini into noodle shape using spiralizer or vegetable grater. Add these zoodles to skillet. Season as desired. Sauté till they have softened, four minutes or so.

6. Toss in the parsley and lemon zest, along with a squeeze of the lemon. Taste and adjust seasoning as desired. Divide into bowls. Top with fish. Garnish as desired and serve.

25 – Squash Salmon with Mojo

Giving the mixture of lime and orange juice a good shot of vinegar gives this dish its citrus flavor. It brings out the taste of the salmon in a wonderful way.

Makes 4 Servings

Cooking + Prep Time: 1 1/2 hours

Ingredients:

- 1 halved 1-pound squash
- 1 head of cauliflower, small, sliced in florets
- 1 wedge-cut onion, red
- 5 tbsp. of oil, olive + extra to drizzle
- Salt, kosher
- 1 pound of salmon fillets, boneless
- 1/3 cup of pumpkin seeds, raw
- 1 orange, small, juiced
- 2 tbsp. of lime juice, fresh
- 2 tbsp. of vinegar, unseasoned rice
- 2 tbsp. of miso, white
- 2 thin-ring-sliced chilies, serrano, small

Instructions:

1. Arrange the racks in upper lower thirds of your oven. Preheat it to 425F.

2. Scoop seeds from the squash. Cut it lengthways in 1-inch strips, then crossways in 1-inch pieces. Toss onions, cauliflower and squash and 3 tbsp. of oil on rimmed cookie sheet. Use kosher salt to season. Roast on the top rack of oven and toss occasionally till veggies are tender and browned fully, 25 to 30 minutes.

3. Reduce the temperature of oven to 300F. Lightly drizzle salmon with olive oil. Season with salt, all over. Then, push the vegetables over to one side of cookie sheet. Place salmon on other side.

4. Spread the pumpkin seeds on another rimmed cookie sheet. Bake the salmon and veggies on the lower rack till fish is barely firm in middle and opaque. Bake the pumpkin seeds on the top rack till golden, 10-15 minutes.

5. Whisk lime juice, orange juice, miso, vinegar and last 2 tbsp. of oil in small mixing bowl till the miso has dissolved. Add in chilies and stir. Season as desired.

6. Break the salmon in large-sized pieces. Arrange veggies on platter. Top with the salmon. Use dressing to drizzle. Sprinkle with the pumpkin seeds. Serve.

26 – Baked Cod with Basil Tomatoes

This recipe is an easy, quick dinner, even on weeknights. It's gluten-free, delicious and healthy, too.

Makes 4 Servings

Cooking + Prep Time: 1/2 hour

Ingredients:

- 3 tbsp. of oil, olive
- 2 cups of tomatoes, grape or cherry
- 1 1/4 pounds of cod fillets, cut in four to six pieces, 1" thick or thicker
- Kosher salt, ground pepper red chili flakes, as desired
- 1 sliced lemon with zest removed and set aside
- 3 roughly chopped cloves of garlic
- 1/4 cup of torn basil leaves

Instructions:

1. Preheat the oven to 400F.

2. Pour oil into 13" x 9" baking dish and scatter with cloves of garlic. Add tomatoes. Add lemon slices. Toss lightly. Move tomatoes and lemons to one side of pan.

3. Pat fish dry. Place in dish. Turn, coating both sides with olive oil. Spread garlic and tomato mixture back out. Nestle fish into the mixture. Season as desired.

4. Bake at 400F for 10 minutes or so. Using oven mitts, shake pan a little to jostle the tomatoes. Scatter with the lemon zest. Bake for five minutes more, till fish is done as you desire.

5. Add basil leaves and toss them with warm tomatoes so they wilt. Use for garnish and serve promptly.

27 – Crispy Bass with Kohlrabi Salad

The fish in this recipe has a nutty sauce and perfectly crispy skin that **Makes** it taste decadent. If you have the time to toast the nuts yourself, the dish is even more fresh and flavorful, but roasted nuts from the store will serve you well if you don't have spare time.

Makes 4 Servings

Cooking + Prep Time: 1 hour

Ingredients:

- 1 tsp. of honey, pure
- 1/4 cup + 2 tsp. of lemon juice, fresh
- 3 tbsp. of oil, olive
- 1 tsp. of salt, kosher + extra as desired
- 2 peeled, halved lengthways, sliced crossways kohlrabi, small
- 1 quartered, then thinly sliced green apple, large
- 1/2 thinly-sliced onion, red
- 4 x 5 to 6-oz. sea bass fillets (can sub salmon), skin-on
- Pepper, ground
- 1/2 cup of hazelnuts, chopped and blanched
- 6 tbsp. of butter, unsalted, cut in pieces

To serve: lemon wedges

Instructions:

1. Whisk 2 tbsp. of oil, 1/4 cup of lemon juice, honey and a tsp. of kosher salt in large sized bowl. Add onion, kohlrabi and apple. Toss and coat. Allow to set while cooking fish.

2. Swirl the last 1 tbsp. of oil in non-stick skillet and coat. Generously season the fish on each side with kosher salt ground pepper. Place in the cold skillet with skin side facing down.

3. Set on med. heat. Cook till the fat begins cooking out of the fish, four minutes or so. Press gently on the fillets with spatula to ensure good contact between pan and fish skin. Continue to press and cycle from one fillet to next every couple seconds, till the skin begins crisping.

4. Discontinue pressing and continue cooking till skin has become very crisp and the flesh is mainly opaque, 8 to 10 minutes in total. Turn the fillets over. Cook till fully opaque, one minute or so. Place the fish with skin side facing up on individual plates.

5. Wipe skillet out. Return it to med. heat. Cook the hazelnuts in butter. Swirl the pan often, till the butter is foamy, then browns, four minutes or so. Remove pan from heat. Stir in last 2 tsp. of lemon juice. Season the browned butter sauce with kosher salt and ground pepper.

6. Toss the kohlrabi salad. Serve alongside the fish fillets and add dressing. Spoon the butter sauce on fish and salad. Serve with lemon wedges to squeeze.

28 – Salmon Mushroom Bowl

In this delicious recipe, the salmon and mushrooms play off each other's flavors in a wonderful way. You can serve it over rice or cabbage.

Makes 2 Servings

Cooking + Prep Time: 35 minutes

Ingredients:

For salmon

- 1 to 2 tbsp. of oil, sesame
- A pinch each of kosher salt, ground pepper red pepper flakes
- 2 pieces of salmon, thick (8 to 10 oz. total weight)
- 4 oz. of de-stemmed, sliced mushrooms, shiitake

For the Sauce

- 3 tbsp. of soy sauce, reduced sodium
- 3 tbsp. of mirin
- 1 tbsp. of Furikake Japanese-type seasoning

For assembly

- 1 1/2 to 2 cups of nicely cooked rice, quinoa or black rice
- 2 large handfuls of cabbage, shredded
- 1 sliced avocado

For garnishing: scallions, Furikake seasoning, cucumber, chili flakes

Instructions:

1. If using rice, cook and prepare.

2. Mix mirin and soy sauce in small sized bowl.

3. Heat oil in large, heavy skillet on med-high. Season as desired and swirl together. Add mushrooms and salmon. Sear each side till golden in color.

4. Turn the heat off. Allow skillet to cool a bit so the sauce doesn't burn. Spoon the sauce over tops of mushrooms and salmon and swirl. Set aside.

5. Divide rice into two individual bowls. Sprinkle with Japanese seasoning. Arrange avocado wedges and cabbage in bowls. Top with mushrooms and salmon. Sprinkle with Japanese seasoning again. Spoon remainder of sauce over cabbage and avocado. Serve promptly.

29 – Grilled Sesame Salmon

Using all the parts of the lemon in this sauce gives it a great texture and brightness. The honey offsets any bitterness, and the balance **Makes** it a natural to complement salmon.

Makes 4 Servings

Cooking + Prep Time: 1 hour 5 minutes

Ingredients:

- 4 x 6-oz. salmon fillets, removed pin bones, patted dry, skin-on
- 2 tbsp. + 1/3 cup of oil + extra for the grill
- Salt, kosher
- 1 lemon, small
- 1 chopped shallot, small
- 2 tsp. of sesame seeds, black
- 1 tsp. of honey, pure
- 1/2 tsp. of sesame oil, toasted
- Pepper, ground
- 1 cup of basil leaves, torn

Instructions:

1. Prepare grill for med. heat. Rub the salmon using 2 tbsp. of oil. Season each side with kosher salt.

2. Cut lemon ends off. Discard ends. Place lemon standing upright. Slice outer lobes off in four sections. Leave the core and seeds. Chop lobes finely and transfer into small sized bowl. Squeeze juice out of core over the bowl.

3. Add remainder of olive oil, sesame oil, honey, sesame seeds and shallots. Season with kosher salt and plenty of ground pepper. Toss, combining well.

4. Clean grill grate and oil it. Place salmon immediately on grill with the skin side facing down. Cover. Cook, leaving skin side facing down the whole time, till skin chars lightly and fish becomes opaque, six to eight minutes. Transfer the salmon to plate. Allow to cool a bit.

5. Divide the salmon among individual plates and top them with basil. Spoon the sesame-lemon sauce over the top. Serve.

30 – Brazilian Fish Coconut Stew

This fish stew originated in Brazil, where it's known as Moqueca. The fish is simmered in rich coconut milk, along with lime, chilies, tomatoes and onions. It's a great dish, filled with wonderful flavors.

Makes 4 Servings

Cooking + Prep Time: 40 minutes

Ingredients:

For fish

- 1 to 1 1/2-lbs. of white fish, firm, like bass, cod or halibut – thicker is better
- 1/2 tsp. of salt, sea
- 1 fresh lime, juice and zest only

For stew

- 2 to 3 tbsp. of oil, olive or coconut
- 1 diced onion, red
- 1/2 tsp. of salt, sea + extra as desired
- 1 cup of diced carrots
- 1 diced bell pepper, red
- 4 roughly chopped cloves of garlic
- 1/2 diced jalapeno pepper
- 1 tbsp. of tomato paste, low sodium
- 2 tsp. of paprika, sweet
- 1 tsp. of cumin, ground
- 1 cup of stock, chicken or fish
- 1 1/2 cups of diced tomatoes, fresh
- 1 x 14-oz. can of milk, coconut (solids and liquids)
- 1/2 cup of parsley, cilantro or scallions, chopped
- 1 squeeze from lime, fresh

Instructions:

1. Rinse the fish and pat it dry. Cut in two-inch pieces and place them in medium bowl. Add sea salt, 1/2 lime zest and 1 tbsp. fresh lime juice. Then massage fish lightly, coating all pieces. Set fish aside.

2. In large-sized sauté pan, heat oil on med-high. Add onions and sea salt. Sauté for two to three minutes. Reduce heat to med. Add jalapeños, garlic, bell peppers and carrots. Cook for four to five minutes more.

3. Add stock, tomato paste and spices. Mix. Bring to simmer. Add the tomatoes. Cover pan. Gently simmer over med-low heat for five minutes, till carrots have become tender. Add coconut milk. Taste and adjust seasonings as desired.

4. Nestle fish in stew. Gently simmer till cooked fully through, four to six minutes. Spoon broth over fish. Cook till fish is done as you desire. Taste and season again as desired.

5. Serve on rice, sprinkled with scallions or cilantro and squeeze from lime.

Conclusion

This fish cookbook has shown you...

How to use different ingredients to affect unique and wonderful tastes in fish dishes both well-known and rare.

How can you include fish recipes in your home repertoire?

You can...

- Make new potatoes and snapper, which you may not have had before. They are just as tasty as they sound.
- Learn to cook with lemon and sesame, which are widely used in fish recipes. Find them in local food markets.
- Enjoy making the most delectable seafood dishes, including salmon, mackerel and cod. Fish is a mainstay in healthy eating, and there are SO many ways to make it great.
- Make dishes using bell peppers and mushrooms, which are often used in fish recipes.
- Make various types of seafood like trout and tilapia, which will tempt your family's appetite.

Have fun experimenting! Enjoy the results!

About the Author

Allie Allen developed her passion for the culinary arts at the tender age of five when she would help her mother cook for their large family of 8. Even back then, her family knew this would be more than a hobby for the young Allie and when she graduated from high school, she applied to cooking school in London. It had always been a dream of the young chef to study with some of Europe's best and she made it happen by attending the Chef Academy of London.

After graduation, Allie decided to bring her skills back to North America and open up her own restaurant. After 10 successful years as head chef and owner, she decided to sell her business and pursue other career avenues. This monumental decision led Allie to her true calling, teaching. She also started to write e-books for her students to study at home for practice. She is now the proud author of several e-books and gives private and semi-private cooking lessons to a range of students at all levels of experience.

Stay tuned for more from this dynamic chef and teacher when she releases more informative e-books on cooking and baking in the near future. Her work is infused with stores and anecdotes you will love!

Author's Afterthoughts

I can't tell you how grateful I am that you decided to read my book. My most heartfelt thanks that you took time out of your life to choose my work and I hope you find benefit within these pages.

There are so many books available today that offer similar content so that makes it even more humbling that you decided to buying mine.

Tell me what you thought! I am eager to hear your opinion and ideas on what you read as are others who are looking for a good book to buy. Leave a review on Amazon.com so others can benefit from your wisdom!

With much thanks,

Allie Allen

Printed in Great Britain
by Amazon

62635610R00052